Praise for 52 ways back home

"Beccy provides a very clear and heartfelt journey for everyone through her very expressive self.

Gently stirring and collaborating all of what life has gifted her own soul and sharing these very intimate truths with us all.

Simply spoken straight to your heart.

Easy to use chapter at a time or purely invoke the learnings and open a random page.
52 ways back home nurses your heart and soul to all that you have signed up for at this time of earthly living.
It gives you some amazing skills to help navigate life's unknowns. No matter how difficult the crossing, you will find your answers to keep going.

It takes great wisdom and knowing to write and share your journey of love and Beccy has magically coloured her unfolding through her awareness of nature's gifts."

Melinda Smith, Psychotherapist, counsellor and healer

———————

"I loved it.
You've just given me the nudge I needed to make my

morning walks a regular thing instead of scraping in more time in bed which I have been doing - because they are my meditations too!
I can't imagine anyone not feeling connected with your soulful words by the end of the introduction, as I was.

Such simple questions that then become tools for transformation, realising bad habits and shifting into a better version of Self. Love it.

Your words provoked old dreams to move back out of the depths and be re-ignited with now.

One of my faves was the great tips to get through the discomfort of "When you are growing".
I can imagine many readers moving and growing with your words."

Nicole Whiteman, Yoga, Pilates & Meditation teacher, Master Trainer of Yogalates ™

52 WAYS BACK HOME

ALSO BY BECCY HOWE

*Arriving Home: Finding your heart and soul again after
a long break*
Book II in the Home series

Being cards set
Simple watercolour paintings to meditate on

Visit **www.beccyhowe.com** for more information

Book I in the Home series

52 WAYS BACK HOME

*How five simple minutes a week can
change your life for the better*

BY BECCY HOWE

Sydney, Australia

Disclaimer: This book is not intended to replace medical or theraputic care. If you have experienced stress or trauma or have any health concerns or issues please seek appropriate professional support. This book is about my own personal experience and may not be right for you. It is up to you and your own doctor or therapist to decide that.

First edition: June 2018
Publisher: Green Rainbows House, Sydney, Australia.
Contact books@beccyhowe.com Printing information on last pages.
To order more copies email books@beccyhowe.com or
visit www.beccyhowe.com/books or contact your local book seller.

National Library of Australia Cataloguing-in-Publication entry (hbk)
Creator: Howe, Rebecca, author.
Title: 52 ways back home : how five simple minutes a week can change your life for the better / By Beccy Howe.
ISBN: 9780648063114 (hardback)
Series: Home series ; bk I.
Subjects: Self-actualization (Psychology) Stress management.
Reflection (Philosophy)

Paperback ISBN: 978-0-6480634-0-7
Hardback (Gift edition, vibrant colour) ISBN: 978-0-6480634-1-4
Ebook ISBN: 978-0-6480634-2-1

Cover design by LisaArts and Green Rainbows House
Chapter closing illustrations © 2016 Beccy Howe
Photographs © 2015 Beccy Howe
Author photograph by Emma Wand Photography

Dedication

I dedicate this book to my beautiful family and all the natural world around me. Without you this work would never have seen the light of day.

How to use this book

This book is not meant to be read from start to finish in one sitting. Feel free to do that if you would like to but you will probably miss its maximum benefit.

The introduction is a great place to start the first time.

I then recommend pausing for a moment or two, perhaps take a slow breath in and out, and try one of the following:

1. Open a page at random, or
2. Scan through the contents pages and see which title stands out or draws you, or
3. Pick a number from 1 to 52 and read that piece.

(Each chapter has 13 pieces so Chapter 1 has 1-13, Chapter 2 has 14-26, Chapter 3 has 27-39 and Chapter 4 has 40-52.)

Find your own way. You know it all already.

Enjoy the journey. x

Contents

Foreword

I suppose I have known Beccy for most of the decade that she says she has been consciously in the healing business; what she calls the health and therapy field. I am sure that the roots, trunk, branches, leaves and flowers, that have taken form in this very attractive book come from the seed of a life that is now only beginning to blossom into maturity. There is a forest to come from Beccy herself and from those, whether clients or students, that she will inspire.

In the decade of our relationship, roles have been teacher, supervisor, student and friend. At 86 I rather forget who was which and am happy to leave it that way.

52 Ways Back Home is a profoundly simple book; or simply profound; according to your taste.

Beccy gives us a series of reflections to look at in the mirror that she holds up to us. One for each week of the year. She gently invites us to honesty and from honesty, to awareness and from awareness, to the possibility of empowerment. We do not get fixed. We expand into our natural true selves that are unimaginable to the limitations of our habituations.

Sensation, feeling, thinking and intuition are all there and presented with a vulnerability which invites us to find our own. This is not a didactic book; it comes from Beccy's experience – her journey. Signposts are there to help us find and keep on our own path. I join her in asking you to take it.

Presence, listening, feeling, relationship, love, trust, intelligence (yes, and the intellect!) are all in evidence; as are their opposites.

The illustrations generously and appropriately ease us into sensation and feeling. It is a cohesive and rounded story. The outer reflects the inner, and the reverse. It is meditation and compassion and action.

Yes! You are good enough. Be that! Read the book and find out how to get back home to who you really are.

Mike Boxhall RCST FCSTA
Director of The Empty Chair Teaching Foundation

Introduction

When I was 12 my father died, suddenly, in a helicopter crash.

I 'knew' this was bad, was big, was upsetting but over the years as I grew I think I got 'busy'.

I had "things to get done". Things that were far more pressing, urgent important.

People told me, advised me to "Just feel it." To "Sit still." "Why don't you ...?" So obvious, so simple, so *easy*, to them. So easy.

Over time I grew. Physically, professionally, emotionally and mentally. My career took off ironically, maybe obviously, in caring for others. My aim became to help *others* feel good. Feel well. Like *themselves*.

I didn't know, really wasn't conscious *at all*, of what was going on inside of me.

I really *was* too busy. This thing really *was* too 'important' / 'urgent' / 'valuable'.

To care for them. To fix that. To improve ....

I honestly, consciously anyway, didn't know that I was holding so much, carrying so much pain, fear, intense emotion.

I "got stuff done" sure. I progressed. I grew. I 'succeeded'. Sometimes did amazing things. But, but, but. My tendency was still to be busy. To move, to rush perhaps. To not sit still for long, or certainly not to feel

1

deeply and "be in my body" as so many fellow adults, carers, supervisors advised.

Yes I 'achieved'. Yes I felt good. But how was I on the inside?

In 2015 I found myself with time on my hands. No obvious big goal to achieve. No obvious big place to go or be. I loved my family dearly and I loved where and how we were living. I felt, and was, and am, so blessed, so lucky in so many ways.

This time though, this time something was different. Something was different.

I found myself going on early morning walks. Initially as a way of ticking some boxes (exercise, meditation etc). Meeting some of my then missing needs as a mum.

I told myself that these times would *achieve* x, y and z.

I had official, reasonable excuses. It was OK. I could go.

As I awoke each morning and started my walks I found myself using this opportunity as a way to get back in touch with me.

To dare to glimpse at myself.

Only out of the corner of my eye to start with. But as I got braver, as I started to *feel* the benefits, started to *come home to myself*, I realised that maybe, just maybe *this was actually useful*.

That I *could* love me on the inside too.

That I *could* honour *me too*. *That I could dare to feel* and that maybe *that was good*.

INTRODUCTION

As I lay listening to my alarm, as I walked outdoors in the silence and aloneness of the early morning, I realised that answers were coming too. Insights, ideas, thoughts and a feeling of peace that seemed to be coming from such a loving feeling place. A place of kindness, of wisdom. Of understanding.

That it was OK, *that I was ok*, just as I am now. With all this perceived gunk. With all my perceived ideals, failures, wishes, hopes and dreams. *With me. With me already.*

I started to write them down.
I was doing a great productivity course at the time so already had an easy way of doing this on my phone. I put it on airplane mode and silent so I could focus, be with only what I chose to. Only what I dared to or felt *brave enough* to.

And then, then, I would just sit, and feel, and walk and feel, and pause and explore and feel. In my mind, my heart, even my soul perhaps. (Whatever that means to you dear reader. I hope, I would love that you keep reading these words.)

As I wrote and later re-read these words, this kind loving accepting sense re-arose. I gained *more* insights, *more* peace, more of a sense of love and ok-ness. *It was OK to be just me, to feel this after all. Somehow a sense came that I am not alone. I am OK.* Not only that I am

OK and capable on the inside, but with all these feelings, grief, guilt, despair too.

I am OK.

This became such a precious part of my day, my life even. It became a time where I could *truly be myself.* I could be honest with, and accepting of, me. With *all that that meant* in this moment.

Each moment I spent.

And as I wrote I would sometimes share, with my partner, with like-minded friends, with peers too.

And I noticed a strange thing. *They seemed to benefit too. To feel the same uplifted peaceful sense too.*

Each writing was on a different topic, yes. But *they all seemed useful.*

And so, and so the idea formed. To share these, to share these with you too dear reader. To share these with others who are also "too busy", too many things to do first.

Or just plain "don't want to" read, to feel, to listen, to sense into icky, yucky upsets from the past. From inside? No thank you very much.

These words seemed to have come into relatively small chunks. Chunks that *can be easily read in a minute or two.*

Chunks that *don't take much from your day but, but, but, can maybe give you something.*

Some peace, awareness, maybe even a new direction.
Perhaps a place to come to when you, like millions do I'm
sure, feel a bit down, a bit lost, uncertain maybe.
A point in your day, in your *life*, where you *could maybe
get some peace*. A *moment* to reflect. To go in and *love
you*.

My wish is that in sharing these, others may touch on or
in this place also, with hopefully also that feeling of love
and ok-ness too.
Even if only for a moment. Even if only for now.
Even if only for today.

Give this to yourself. Give this to your family. Then give
this to your world around you.
It's so simple to read some words. It's only a minute or
two isn't it?

Could you pick a page now and go in? Start, begin, to
love you now, honor you now, *if only for a minute*.

This doesn't have to be big. It doesn't have to be grand
even. You don't have to tell anyone else.
Just do this for you now.
Put this book in your pocket, your home, your bedside
table or workspace, maybe your car.
And just go in, one day, one week at a time.

You are worth it.
You are.

Chapter 1

Finding your birds

Have you ever looked up into a big tree to find the bird that is singing? The source of that noise that is filling, distracting you from, the peace and silence underneath and all around you?

What is your bird?

Is it a memory, how you experienced an event in your life? Something someone said when you were ...?

FINDING YOUR BIRDS

You can't often see your bird straight away. How hard do you look? Is it hiding around the back, blocked slightly by someone else's tree? Or is it so clear, moving and bobbing around, that it's right in front of you. Full face on. No avoiding this one.

That's often when the tears are there. The strong emotions that have broken through our defences. The strong emotions that are no longer hidden behind branches we've created to cope in the world. When these issues wobble and are BAM right here, in our heart, our mind, then you know it's time.

"*Please listen!*" your body says, your heart begs.

If you're lucky, it's all convenient. Your friends, support, are right there. Often times though, these feelings come up when it's not convenient. When we *don't want to* cry, feel, wobble.

You may also have a sense that there are birds somewhere in your tree but you can't see them clearly.

You may need to be quiet, become still and allow them to show themselves to you in their own way, their own time.

Can you be with this waiting, allowing, not knowing while they may or may not show themselves? Can you take a step back, look at the whole tree? See how it is supported, nourished?

CHAPTER 1

Maybe light, clarity, is affected a little by those around it? Or our perception of them affecting us, blocking us anyway. Can you see how there is still light and nourishment possible for it?

Can you ask anyone else, a trusted friend or professional, to help you to see more clearly? A different perspective can often help.

Sometimes you can see the birds clearly. Sometimes you have to go looking for them, to understand what may be blocking you from the peace you crave.

These birds - these thoughts, perceptions and ideals - may or may not be useful to you anymore. But they will, at least at first, feel like part of your tree, your identity.

Please remember that they came into existence to try and help you. To protect you. My experience is that they are *always* trying to help in some way. They may just have formed at a time when you didn't have as much life experience or clarity, or were already full of stuff to deal with.

With some help, time and patience, the ones that are useful to the tree stay. The ones that no longer serve it, will fly away.

They do, and will, if you can accept, love and thank them, allow them.

Then more light can come in and, if you're lucky, peacefulness can be yours for a while.

The birds are useful. The tree is useful.

All the wonderful branches you have grown are useful. It's *all* part of life.

And you can still be your tree, still feel the air on your branches, the earth under and around you.

And let the birds sing too.

Being, accepting & loving what is already

Can you be in this moment?

Can you accept what you see in front of you and, more importantly, what you are feeling right now?
Can you allow the quietness to come up ... and then, after a time, the quiet voices that come too?

BEING, ACCEPTING & LOVING WHAT IS ALREADY

Those voices that can guide you in your day, your lifetime if you'll let them. Those voices that, when you were a child, gave you inspiration for imaginary games to play, ideas for exploring and spontaneous laughter.
Those voices are still with you, still reachable. But you need to find, no - to allow, the quietness to arise *first*.

Can you find a space in your day today, a place where you can pause and reflect?
A place to listen to that initially-very-busy trail of thoughts, worries and ideas?

This could be at the familiar traffic lights you pass every day, a moment to look down at the ground whilst others are distracted around you, even sitting in the bathroom or brushing your hair in the mirror.

Yes, the mirror is a very good place to start loving yourself - more on that later.

But for now, for today, give yourself the blessing of a few minutes of quiet, a space to be, to feel and, with time, *to love what is there already.*

Do you see your life has already started?

Warning: this one is forthright and perhaps a bit confronting. It's meant to be. I want *you* to wake up and see that *you* are important. *You* matter. And *your* honest wellbeing is needed on this planet, in your life, as much as anyone else's.

Take a deep breath, have a drink of water and read on ...

———

Do you see that your life has already started?

Can you see that you are here, on earth, already?

DO YOU SEE YOUR LIFE HAS ALREADY STARTED?

What are you doing now?
Are you really respecting, honouring and caring for yourself? Not necessarily right now, but today, in *your* life.

Can you remember what *you* enjoy? What you *love*?

I myself, forgot how important sleep is. I started a project, loved it, was inspired by it and then stayed up late three nights in a row doing it.
The result? I felt super high at the time, proud of getting on with it, but each morning as I tried to start my day, my energy levels, motivation and joy were getting less.

Are you loving yourself today?

What are your needs?

Pause for a moment if you can.
Look around you.
Follow your own sweet breath in and out, in and out of *your* body, your lungs.

Ask yourself: "What would I *love* today?" "What would nurture *my soul*?" "What, at the end of this day, will have sent a clear message that I love myself?"

Love *yourself* today.

Do something small, easy, that makes *you* feel genuinely good and listened to.

Honour yourself, *then* those around you.

CHAPTER 1

Then the whole world benefits.

Be like the tree trunk

Would you like smooth or rough?
Flowing, soft or scaly, rigid and hard?

Which side of you do you show to others? Are you allowing *their stuff* to penetrate? Or does what they have to say, to think, to *believe* have to pause, intermesh and get stuck and icky in your bark?
This is not who you are. *This* is only a perception.

CHAPTER 1

A place where you see and form your identity. "*This* is who *I* am." "*This* is all I can be now."

Is it? Is it really? Can you *feel* how deep this goes inside of you? Do you know who and what you *really* are?
Is this bark, this show you put on, a defence you put up, *all* that you are?

Can you remember a time when this *wasn't* the case?
A time when you felt joy and happiness and peace?

Do you have to take on *this*? Does it have to integrate, and mesh with old 'stuff'?
Old beliefs that no longer serve you but you hold onto them anyway. This bark, this outer seemingly-protective layer has become so unnoticed, so familiar, in your I'm-too-busy-to-sit-down-and-feel-this life that you forget it ever was a choice.

There are trees all around you. They *all* have their own experiences and, most importantly, their *memories*, *their interpretations*, of these experiences.

How we see, hear and feel something, how we believe the situation to be, how we think we are at fault, or not, can all have a huge impact on what we do with this in our subconscious.

Where do we store this idea, how and why?
How do we link it, justify it, play it out later? Who will trigger us?

BE LIKE THE TREE TRUNK

And trigger *this* particular memory or belief, this way of interpreting the world?

Will I show you my rough and sticky bark or my smooth I-don't-care-what-you-think layer? (By don't-care, I don't mean that this comes from a place of defensiveness, but rather a sense of inner connection and self-acceptance that does not *need* anything, or anyone on the 'outside' to *be* any different.)

Can you be who you are today? Can you observe your rough/smooth bark?
Can you feel your trunk? Could you consider that you even *are* the trunk?

Can you feel, if only for a few moments, where the stickiness, the roughness is?
Is it possible to let that thought, that word, *their* comments, slide off or past?
Could you experiment with doing this? "How am I responding, reacting to this person? To this situation? Can I allow *anything* to flow just now?
Here, in *this moment*, this *one situation*, can I let these thoughts and ideas just slide on past me?
Do I *really* need to pick up this and hold onto to it, react to it, let it irritate me and get stuck, let it affect or disturb me right now?"

Play with this for a day or two. See, listen and feel how you feel, how it is in each moment for *you*.

CHAPTER 1

Then you will be getting closer to home. To that peace you have been searching for, *for so long.*

You *are* already home. You *are* already ok. Maybe you just forgot and were looking at the bark, instead of this beautiful inner tree?

An opening flower

What stage of opening are you at today?
Can you see the light around you?
Can you feel the raindrops, feel life, on your leaves or petals?

Now is the time to blossom, to risk knowing and being who you are. Yes, you can stay small, or you can rise and open up to this light.
What stage do you feel like today?

Do you need to be the bud, curled up quiet, in your own world for a while? Perhaps a time of inward looking and pondering is called for. A time to reflect on where you are - and indeed how you are - at this moment, this part of *your* life.

There is no need to be the flower that someone else appears as, to *you*.
There is only a need to reconnenct and to re-familiarise yourself *with* yourself. *Your* self, *your* soul and *your* life's journey. *Whatever that may mean for you now.*

Yes, there can be times when daring to open, to blossom, to shine are just the perfect things for you.

Yes, it can be fun and beautiful to radiate outwards, sharing your gifts and petals with the world - that they may see and know *your own* flower's perfume.

Yes, this can be fun and exciting.

But, and this is a big but, you *cannot* push to be amazing *every day*. Every day is not the same. You come with different issues, needs, wishes and, of course, different people and issues around you.
Let's just start with today.

What is it you need *today, right now*? What would you *love* to have achieved or experienced by the end of this day, this time?
Start small, one little petal at a time.

What do you need right now?

AN OPENING FLOWER

This can be as simple as a deep breath in, or out. A drink, a hug, a few minutes in the sun or to dance like no-one's watching. To go for a big fun spontaneous run with a buddy, or alone.

See if you can tune in to what *you* need and then, with a little courage, focus and practice, you can really bring yourself home.

And the flower is exactly how, and where, it needs to be.

Tomorrow is another day, different weather and light levels.

Think only of today for now.

I can choose. So can you

What would you like to do with *your* life?

Do you know that you can start it already? That you don't actually *have* to wait until "The timing is right", "I have enough support", "No-one else is doing anything else like it".

Do you know that you can be *yourself* and you *don't need* to change anything dramatically? Just be more of you. As you are now. As you *can* be, if you let your consciousness settle into your own body, warts and all. Blessings and all. Yukky icky sticky resisting bits and all.

Can you be here now at this point in your life and know that you are enough already?

You ... are ... enough ... already.

You. Yes, you. I wasn't talking to, or about, anyone behind you.

Can you take that first step forward? Even if you are not sure exactly where it might lead?

Can you settle into your own body, into its sensations? Settle into those inner yearnings and cries that don't get listened to often? Maybe only in the occasional massage, or nature walk, or unexpected silent moment on a holiday?

Do you know where you want to go yet? If not, *that's ok.* If we knew all that was ahead of us we might not allow, believe it is 'for us'.

We can *only* start with what is here, inside of us, in front of us.

Our needs now.

Can you first feel, tune into your needs, wishes, hopes and fears? As they are now, here, in your body at *this* moment.

And *then* begin. *Then* start. *Then begin to come home.*

CHAPTER 1

When was the last time you stopped to smell the roses?

When was the last time you stopped to 'smell the roses'? Can you remember? What does that mean *to you*?

Do you tend to look at the positives in life? Or the negatives?
Can you even remember what and how you look?
Has it all become such a habit that you have absolutely no idea, no reference?

Then maybe it's time to just sit with your thoughts.

Figuratively speaking, as in watching, observing them as you go about your day. Or actually sitting with them.

CHAPTER 1

Find a quiet spot to sit alone, perhaps have a notepad and pen with you. Create two columns. "Positives" and "Negatives". Get curious.

Ask yourself: "What are my thoughts about my job? My partner? My family? My home? The people I meet each day? The state of the world in general?"

Start to notice what comes up *for you.*

No need to share this with anyone if you don't want to. Let's just keep this private, really open and honest. Keep asking and keep writing these thoughts in one of the two columns. Negatives and Positives.

When you've written down *everything* you can think of, try this. For each statement in the Negatives column, can you turn it around? Can you see if you can find one positive in the situation? Something that feels good?

There must be something somewhere or you wouldn't have ever allowed them in your life to start with, subconsciously or otherwise. Can you see what *that* is?

Is it perhaps time to consider another way of thinking? Of seeing? Of *speaking*?

What we say out loud can be powerful and really affect our emotions, our sense of self. Watch this especially.

Maybe play with this today. Watch your thoughts, what you say. Perhaps start with when you are about to leave the house. About to go into your workplace. About to speak with someone.

What are you bringing with you? What thoughts, judgements and ideas are you starting that situation with? *Can* you play with the opposite? Perhaps an absolutely tiny change at first but then, *given time, practice and self-kindness*, can this new idea become more familiar in your day? In your life?

Do you remember a time when you *did* feel joy, laughter and happiness?

What we think, *what we say*, on a day to day basis will determine how likely those times are to occur again. How often. How possible.

What are you telling your subconscious that you want? What are you telling your subconscious that you see?

What are you telling your subconscious about *your life*? *Do you even want this to be different?*

Is this one thought serving you?
What is this thought, this method of thinking, this habit bringing you?
How do you feel when you think, talk, *feel* like that?
How do you feel when you think, talk, feel the opposite?
That original reason why you allowed, why you created *this* situation or person in your life?

CHAPTER 1

Could you change this if you wanted to? *Do* you want to?

How do you want to feel?
Can you remember?
Can you try to?

Is it possible to play with this today in *your* life, *your* experience, *your* perception?

Maybe you could try?

WHEN WAS THE LAST TIME YOU STOPPED TO SMELL THE ROSES?

Positives   Negatives   Turn it around

From the dark to the light. Are you coming too?

I find some time each day to stop and be in nature.
For this rests my mind - my thoughts. It rests my thinking, worrying, the need to create/fix/make/be or do a certain thing or way.
Is this something *you* would like? If not, what is?
Where could *you* go to be alone for a few minutes each day? Is there somewhere that springs to mind or would

you need to spend a few minutes thinking about it? Go
on, try it now ...

... did you think of somewhere? It could be the local
park, the beach, even your bathroom or looking out a
window.
Could you imagine sitting there today? Tomorrow? Could
you plan this into *your* day?
Go on, think about it for a minute or two now ...

How could this become a reality for you? *How could this
work for you and your particular situation?*

There will be some time, some point, even at the traffic
lights, where you can sit, be, even feel for a minute or
two. Maybe this could extend to 20 minutes, if you play
with it? Maybe *it is time* to play with this *now*?

What difference might it make in *your* life? In *your* day?
In *your* body, mind and soul?

Can you think back to what you wanted from your *life*
and *at what point that started to change for you*? Maybe
you had a baby, changed jobs, started studying, moved
to a new place and forgot?
You got caught up, so focused on the doing, that you
forgot what was happening on the inside? Your plans,
your ideals. Your hopes and wishes?
Where did they go? Did they actually go? Are they still
in there somewhere?

CHAPTER 1

Maybe, just maybe, it's time to check back in and say hi. You may be pleasantly surprised by what you find there.

Are you blocking yourself?

When you think of doing something fun, something exciting, perhaps something you've wanted to do for ages, can you do it easily?

Does it all flow beautifully? Or do you start doing it, maybe even only start thinking of it, and BAM. Emotions, thoughts and worries fill your mind?

What do you say to yourself then? What *are you* saying to yourself? Then and every day?

CHAPTER 1

Can you let an idea come, a thought of new possibilities? Or is the need to stay small, safe in familiar territory, too strong a pull?

What are *you blocking yourself* with?

Could you stretch up into that idea? Could you consider what it might feel like to accomplish that? Even for one second?

Maybe it's time to start dreaming, to start daring, to consider what *you would love.* Love to do, be or create. Love to give, receive or share. Love to see, hear, or know.

What litter, what thoughts, what beliefs and ideals are you throwing in there too?

Sometimes it's not even conscious how and when and why you do this. My feeling is that these thoughts, doubts and fears are *always trying to help you.* Always trying to protect you, in some way.

They were often formed at a time when you didn't have much life experience and could only interpret situations and people's responses in a limited way. Perhaps you took something personally that *was never about you.* Perhaps someone said or did something that was *only about their stuff. Their* feelings, thoughts and beliefs. *Their litter.*

Can you start to see today what is *someone else's stuff, someone else's litter* and *what may be yours?*

ARE YOU BLOCKING YOURSELF?

Can you consider that others have their own blockages? *Their own* ideas, fears, hopes and wishes, limitations. Maybe *that* is why they are reacting like *that*?

Could you start to play with following *your own dreams*? Start to imagine how *that would feel*.

Then, and this is the important bit, *watch and listen to the litter that you throw in*.

Trying to heal another

Have you ever tried to heal someone else's pain?

To try and fix *their* problems?
How does it *feel*? Why are *you* motivated to try and do this?
Is it actually as a way of *you healing yourself*?

Do *you* want to fix *them* so your own heart doesn't hurt so much?

Is it *their* pain, or is it *your own* that you are really trying to heal?
Can you be with your *own* pain? Your *own* sensations?
Your *own* well-being or lack of?

TRYING TO HEAL ANOTHER

Do you ever hear yourself saying, "If I/they can just ... "
"If/when they do ... "
Can you come home to what *you* need right now?

What is *this* (their apparent feelings and experience) ...
what is *this* bringing up for *me*?
How do I *feel* when I think about *them* and *their* situation?
Can I just sit with that? Can I allow my body to talk to me, to tell me what's going on? What *my* body's message is for *me*?

There is no going home from the outside.

There is no going home from another's feelings, emotions and experiences.
However, this can be a *tool*, a useful way, a mirror to access our *own* pain. An opportunity to see and feel and hear how things are for *us*.
Can you dare to do *this*? To look *inside*?

I'm not saying to ignore the other. Only that, when you *are* alone, and you *do* have a moment, maybe, just maybe have a look at what is happening for you.

There may be an opportunity for some growth, some healing, some more space for love and peace and wellbeing for *you* too.

This, if you actually do it, has the great potential to then *really help the other too.*

CHAPTER 1

The clarity and peace you *both* can feel and experience *afterwards* is amazingly healing.

And that's what you want, right?

How good will you let yourself feel?

So you've read 'the' books, done 'the' course, a bit of meditation here and there. But can you let go of what is actually holding you back from experiencing life? Experiencing joy? Happiness? And love?

I had a mixed bag of events and experiences growing up. Some challenges, some joyful loving moments. I've slowly come to realise that it is now *my choice* what I do with them. How I perceive them and which ones I choose to carry forward into each next stage of *my life*.

What can you see when you look back in your life? Were there challenges? Were there moments of joy, of love? Probably? Are you ... can you ... be clear about

CHAPTER 1

that?

How much do you want to?

Is there something, a part, you don't want to connect with?

Perhaps a part that is "better left alone".

Do you know that you even have a choice?

Yes, to first look and *feel*. Yes, to understand you need to first allow memories, *allow feelings and sensations to come up* into your conscious mind. That part of you that *you can be aware of* quite easily. That part where there *seems* to be the most choice.

How does that sound to you? Could you even imagine it? Either way, maybe it's time to explore this.

Maybe it's time to *consider feeling good*, well, happy and content, if only for a few moments.

How would that feel? How would that be?

How good are you willing to *let yourself feel now*?

You have 2 choices in life

You have two choices in life.

Do you want to grow big or stay small?

Do you want to believe in yourself, in your talents, your potential, or do you want to take on your perception of what others think, what others feel about you?

Do you need *this* in your life right now? Do you want to come home to you, and all *you can achieve*?

Or do you want - is it easier, less scary - to stay hidden, little, useless, out of view?

This tree has grown two trunks, two ways to be, to reach for and allow energy for growth. From the earth and the sky. According to its nature, its blueprint perhaps.

Which one will *you* choose?

Do you have two possible ways of being, of feeling, of *living your life* right now? *Could* there be another way than the one you've been operating from *your whole life*? Do you need to sit and feel that for a moment? Wherever you are.

Can you be with these potentials, these potential versions of *you* and *your life*?

Where and, more importantly, *how* would you like to *live your life*? Could you take a step in *that* direction today? Even just to allow yourself to consider, to imagine, to *feel* it?

Maybe this is just a game, a pointless exercise that you-don't-have-time-for. Maybe it is a simple step, a doorway into more light, more joy and more fun in *your* life?

Wouldn't it be interesting to explore?

Go on now, I double dare you ...

Shine or shadow?

What is in your heart?

Did you come here to shine or stay in the shade? What
was *your* plan?

More importantly, what would *you* like *now*?

Do you want to spend your whole life being small, watching on from the sidelines? Or would you *love* to dive in,
feel this expansion, *your full potential* for joy, for abun-
dance, for helping the world to expand too?

What is it you want, sweetheart? Can you dare to look
inside of yourself now?

CHAPTER 1

Could you dare to feel again that same excitement and sense of wonder that you felt as a child?

Not knowing but perfectly ok with trying. With seeing what may happen.

Trying, then coming back to rest, consider, explore mentally, then off and out again.

Would *you* like to *try*?

What about sitting and feeling for a moment or two now? Imagining how *you* would *feel* staying in the shade your whole life.

Feel good?

Then take a moment or two to feel, *really* visualise, how it might be to stand in the light.

To let this light fall on you, to let others' gazes reach you, to let this light penetrate and fill your energy field, (fulfill) your soul perhaps? Maybe?

What might that be like?

How might *that feel* for *you*?

Would you love to express yourself just as you are?
Warts and all. Bliss, skills, talents and all.

Without the limits of your beliefs, ideas of what is possible, what is ok or normal even?

Without the limits of others' (or your perception of others') beliefs, ideas, of what is possible or ok?

SHINE OR SHADOW?

What is it that is in *your heart today?*

Listen to that, consider the options, *then and only then* take a step in the direction *you* want.

What would fill you with joy? Pride? A sense of "Yes! *I did that.*"

Maybe, just maybe, *that's* what you're here to do.
Maybe, just maybe, *that's* what your plan was.

Maybe?

Chapter 2

Stop to look around you

Do you sometimes get so caught up in life's doings, that you don't even notice what is right next to you?

There could be the most beautiful expressive tree, kind words or gorgeous sunrise but if, like many many people in this world, you are rushing and only thinking of where you are going, you will not see them.
You will not hear them. You will not read or absorb them. You will not breathe in their beauty.

There could be a delicious new recipe someone has made, a new drink to try, a few seconds of eye contact and connection. But, if you are in your head, in your doing, your going, your "I must ... ", "I should ... ", they may as well have never existed in your life.

Is *that* what *you* want?

Do you *want* to have a life of *that*?

Or maybe, just maybe, you might like to look around sometimes.

To stop, to pause,
to *notice the beauty that is already in your life.*
Already around you.

Can you let yourself see it, feel it, hear it, receive it?

Can you allow yourself to experience joy, even for one moment?

I'm not talking about the fast-paced, need-more, when-I-get-there or get-that kind of joy.

I mean - as I'm sure you've already experienced - that simple, pure, peaceful, contented, in-the-moment joy. The contented smile inside that comes almost unexpectedly.

That comes when you are *not* rushing, *not* doing *and* not achieving/pushing/forcing/"must work".

Yes, work and effort and focus can be amazingly useful tools for getting things done. For creating beautiful things that can help you, your family, community, even the world.

But maybe it's those quiet moments that make a *life*.

Maybe that's what you are actually looking for?

CHAPTER 2

Just some thoughts.

See what you'd like to do with, or not do with, them.

Take them into your heart for a moment, let them sit there.

Do *they* resonate, *feel right* for *you*?

Or is this just a game? Not really your life? Well not yet anyway.

You'll get round to *that* (peace, joy, fulfillment, appreciating the moment) another time when you're not so ... so ... well, not so *alive*.

Tips for a healthy life (don't let the weeds grow too long)

Tips for a healthy life (don't let the weeds grow too long).

1. Make some time each day to sit quietly with yourself, preferably in the morning so you start your life that day with clarity.

2. Take a shower or bath in the evening to cleanse all those thoughts and worries and doubts you've gathered away from your body.

3. Brush your teeth regularly (had to say that, right?)

4. Meet up with a good friend, partner or other person you like, to enjoy something physical. It could be a walk,

a meal or drink, a chat, a meditation or yoga session. Bond with your community. It's important for your well-being.

5. Take time each hour to breathe, to feel into your lungs. They do a marvellous job for you each and every day of your wonderful life.

6. Laugh. Be with people who bring this out in you, read books, watch funny movies. *Allow* yourself to smile every day. *This* is important too.

7. Don't try so *hard*. Then life will actually be easy.

8. Look at the big picture yes, then do the little things daily that get you towards that. *One* day at a time. You don't *have to*, or even *can you, do it all at once.*

9. It's *ok to change your mind*, to admit that *maybe you made a mistake.* We are *all* learning, growing, developing and discovering. Each and *every day.*
What you know now *you didn't know yesterday. So how could you have done it the other way?* There are lessons and insights and regrets and new chances daily, weekly and monthly.
You don't *have to*, nor indeed *could you,* be whatever it is you call *perfect* in every second.

10. There has to be a 10, right? Well, let's leave that up to you. What do you know that *you need in your life today*, this week? *Your* life, don't worry about anyone

else's, *their* needs, *their* preconceptions, *their* thoughts.
Get quiet, take a breathe and tune in. What is *your*
number 10 on *your* list today?

Have fun. Remember you are *always* learning and growing. Even if it doesn't feel like it at times.

Take care of yourself. Kindness, patience, understanding
are good places to start (and live from).
Allow things to flow ...

Do we need to wait in the unknown?

Do you sometimes have a point in your day, week or life even, where you *just don't know* what to do? Where to go? How to even *be*?

This has happened for me recently. A family member is getting ill. She doesn't seem to want to do much, be much or own much any more.

Do I push and try and *make* something happen? Or do I, *can I even*, just sit and feel for a while?

Sit and feel what it is in *my* heart, *my* needs and *my* wishes and wants that is so influencing this situation? My perspective of it certainly.

Is this outcome that *I* imagine for the best overall?

DO WE NEED TO WAIT IN THE UNKNOWN?

Can I even know this now?
I don't think I can.

Is there something in your life, an area, situation or need, which is not clear?
Where it's not obvious what or even *when* to do something.
A time where you *just don't know* what to do. Could you, for a moment, a day, a few days, just *be with that*?
That feeling, that *unknown* space where *nothing is clear*.
Where you just don't know.
Can you be with that and *trust that what needs to happen will*, in its *own sweet time*?

That maybe, just maybe, knowing *everything beforehand* is *not* useful.

That maybe, just maybe, *before the birth there needs to be a death. Not a physical death as such, maybe just a period of letting go, of acknowledging things as they are today.*
Of understanding that *you don't understand everything right now.*
That you can't see into the future.

And that maybe, *you don't have to.*

And maybe *that is all you do need to know.*

Are you letting someone else's shadow dim you & your brilliance?

When you are close to someone and you spend a bit of time with them, how is your light, your urge to shine and express more of what you are?

Do you let yourself soar? Do you breathe fully?

Do you know *who you are* when you are with others?

Could you ever imagine it being different?

Maybe this happens, as is often the case, with children. Maybe with your parents? Who is it that you are *keeping yourself small for* exactly?

Who will really benefit from this? From you being *little and not shining*?

ARE YOU LETTING SOMEONE ELSE'S SHADOW DIM YOU & YOUR BRILLIANCE?

Where is your light in *this* world? Where are *you*?
Are you indeed here at all?
How much?
Are you willing to 'do the work'? To 'feel the pain'? By that I mean are you willing to be fully present with all your stuff? Your feelings, wants and wishes.
Can you?
Do you ever want to? Could you ever?
Why? Why not?

Whose life is this actually?

Are you being you? Or are you being who *you guess* others want or think you 'should' be?
Doesn't sound like much fun to me.

What about considering, trying, *playing with another way*?

What about, maybe for today, you be in *your* body with *your* feelings and just accept that's how and what things are just now?

That sounds much better, much more appealing. If you actually *want* to live your own life that is? ...

(Just to clarify, I am *not* saying force your wishes and needs on others. *Do not* make your stuff a way of suppressing or dominating another. But, in your *own* body, with your *own* thoughts and needs and wishes, *acknowledge them yourself*. That, that single thing there alone is massive.)

CHAPTER 2

Good luck and enjoy the experiment. I wonder where, or how, it will take you in your life?

Today ... tomorrow too ...

Sometimes there is nothing to fix

Sometimes there is nothing to 'fix'. It just is. Bare ground, unearthed feeling, no obvious *life* or *vibrancy*.

There can be an uncomfortable thought, idea or feeling. You may be *wishing that it wasn't so*.

Maybe something, someone or a situation didn't go how *you planned*.
How you wanted, no hoped, for something else to happen. Life, that event, experience or that moment to go *differently. That was not what I wanted*.

Is it? Was it? *What about now?*

Can you change your perspective, your response to *your perception* of that now?

What are *you* seeing? What are *you feeling* about this? About *that* actually as it is probably already in the past.

Do you still feel the effects? Do you remember when, or even *how* it started? What were *you feeling* just before that moment or experience?

What were your thoughts about? Your feelings, your ideas? Did *they* influence your interpretation at all? And how *you* experienced it?

Maybe, just maybe, we hold onto things that are *not ours to hold.*
Maybe, just maybe, we are holding onto, even identifying with, things and viewpoints that *were never actually real.*

As a child we can take in so many of *others' viewpoints as our own.*
We can see what the adult seems to be feeling or thinking and 'know' that "this must be how things actually are."
Is it?
Was it?
Do you need that anymore?

Is it serving you?

Is it helping you to *live your life fully now*?

SOMETIMES THERE IS NOTHING TO FIX

Where are you in *your* life? Are you on the path you chose or were planning?

Have you even chosen, or planned, or wished? Do you even *consider* that anymore?

Ask yourself:
1. Is this serving me, helping me to grow and blossom in *my life now?*
2. Is this *a match* for who and what *I want to be or live now?*
3. *Can I possibly find another viewpoint on this? Another perspective?*

Was it mainly because I was only a child, only starting out in life with limited experience?
That maybe, just maybe, I'm coming home to myself by *doing this, considering this.*

Maybe, just maybe, *I can recover* from this - however it has been holding me, guiding me, steering me in *my choices* in life.

Do you want to begin to come home to *you*?

Would you *love* to *feel freely* and deeply and *be ok with that, however that is for you now?*

Would you actually like to be free of this burden, this perspective, maybe limitation?

CHAPTER 2

Well then, sweet one, why don't you begin now?

Do you ever feel lonely, like you 'don't fit in'?

Do you ever feel lonely, like you 'don't fit in'?
Do you ever wish that you could *just be like them, or that, or whatever else it is that you are meant to be?*

Maybe you tried hard to fit in when you were young, maybe you're still trying.

There is another way, you know. The way of remembering who you are and what your original plan and intentions were, for *this, your life.*

How can I find *that* out, you ask?
How can I possibly remember *that*?

CHAPTER 2

I am that already, aren't I? ...

Well then, how do you *feel* in your body today?
Are *you* glad to *be in it*?
Are you *happy and joyful* that you get to wake up each morning? And get on with *your* day?

Do you even notice what or how you are feeling as you get out of bed each morning?

Can you remember how it felt to be excited about something? *Your* excitement. *Your idea* of what is fun. For *you now*?

Could you possibly *play with this for one week*?

Could you notice how you feel upon waking? Those first few moments before worries and thoughts and plans start. And then tune in and *feel,* ask yourself, "What is it that I would *truly love* to do today? *What is it that would give me the biggest smile and grin*?"

What would get you dancing, or smiling or saying "Yes!"

Try it. Maybe. This week.

That's only seven days out of *your life.*

Time to let go?

Sometimes we hold on when it's time to let go. Or at least that's how it feels.

Sometimes we *don't want* to move on, to 'grow up', to be brave.

What we actually want in that moment is to hide, to grasp, to *never* let go. "Is this right?" "Is this correct?" "Did I do it all ok?" "Will anything go wrong?" "Did I do it all? Cover it all?"

Can we ever know it's *really* ok?

Do you ever have times where you're just wondering? No pressure, go-with-the-flow kinda days?

CHAPTER 2

Do you then sometimes have moments where you *just don't know*? And *that* can be scary. Where *things can go wrong. I didn't mean it. Why is this happening? To them, to me, to us*?

Who *would* you like to be, *in your life*?

Do you *want to stay small*?

Do you *want to 'grow big'*?
Whatever that means for you now?

Would you *love* to come home to *yourself*? To *your* joy? To *your* wishes and dreams? To what you *used to love to do - or planned to do* anyway?

Could you imagine that, even for a moment? Even for two moments?

What is it exactly that you are holding on to?

Who are you holding on to this for?

Do they even know you are 'doing this' for them? How might they feel if they knew? If you told them - "I'm holding on to this for you."

"*I'm* holding on to *this* for *you* ... "

How do I know?

How do I know which way to be? Which way to go now? How, or what, to feel?

Is it my fault, a problem, my *choice* that things are happening how they are? Or at least *how they seem* to be.

Did I 'do something wrong'? Is this *feeling* 'wrong'?

Should I be somehow different?

At times I feel really clear on what I need, what needs to be 'done'. Then other times there is a sense of loss, of something or someone missing.
Is this real? This *perception*? Or is this just a completely normal part of feeling, of being, of living?

CHAPTER 2

What about these uncomfortable emotions? Should I push them down?
Should I love myself while they are here, knowing that these are more experiences to grow from? To learn from. Maybe in fact, *just to feel.*

Maybe in fact, there is no *thing to do*?
Maybe in fact, there is no *thing to heal*?
There is only what there is *now, in this moment. My moment, my body.*

Is this easy to understand? Easy to accept, to allow?
Could I possibly know that I don't actually know? That it is indeed ok *not to know.*
Not to change, to fix, to move, to create something new straight away.

Can I be with *how things are just now*?
These feelings? These I-don't-know-what-to-do-with icky emotions.

Is it, maybe, just maybe, ok to just feel? Just be?
No need to rush onto the next 'thing' or achievement?

But instead to sit, just sit, and feel and acknowledge. And sit.

It is what it is, now. Today. For and in *my* life, just for today.

And that, maybe just that, is the *most effective and powerful thing I can do for me now.*

HOW DO I KNOW?

Who are you being now?

Do you ever feel a time, an occasion, a pressure to *be something else*? To act as someone else does, *or at least appears to be*?

When I'm alone it's easier to be clear, to feel clear. When I'm with others it's harder. There is a pull to fit in, to blend in, to connect perhaps.

Can I be with, observe this pull? Maybe it's straight away, maybe a few minutes in. Maybe it's not until the end of my day or even year that I can get perspective. I look back and get to see what is *me*, what is *mine*, what is *them*.

WHO ARE YOU BEING NOW?

How do you define yourself?
Do you identify with the group, the white flowers in the picture?
Are you bold and brave sometimes and dare to be pink? Front and centre. "Here I am. It's *me*."

Perhaps you need, you *wish*, to blend in for the time being. *Maybe that's completely ok for you now.*

If it is, then great. If it isn't, then also great.

What do *you want*?

What do *you need*?

Do you need to shine, to stand out, to *be real*? Or would you actually right now thank-you-very-much, *love* to be in your circle of white flowers. And that is completely ok too.

Take time to feel today. Where would *you like to be? How do you want to express today?*

Is this a time to blend in, to flow, to be part of something that welcomes and accepts you as you are already? A connection already made and it feels good?

Or, and this can change easily from day to day, *is this a time to expand your horizons? To stand out and be seen, be heard? To dare to shine?*

CHAPTER 2

Do what feels right *today*. And only today. Tomorrow brings more insights, more lessons, more clarity.

For now, and only now, think of *how you want to be today.*

Enjoy the journey. xx

Going with the flow

What is it I am here to do? Where *should* I be going?
Doing? Being? Who am I? Where am I?

Do you ever find yourself asking these questions? Silently
in your head. Wondering. It was all so clear last night/week/at
that meeting.

When you are 'walking your path' things can often feel
crystal clear. Ahh, that feels good.
Often though too, things can feel muddled, unclear. Maybe
lost without a clear sense of *where I go now.*

It is then, and often only then, that the good stuff happens, where real growth, new beginnings can be. New

ideas, new wonderments, new beliefs, new *maybe-I-can-do-this* thoughts are birthed.

What ideas would *you* like to express today? Or even in your life generally?

Do you know which direction to take already?

If not, then just sit with it for a while. Go out into the garden, a park, the bush or forest. Get out where there aren't many, or ideally any, people. Somewhere you can be by yourself and just *sit with your stuff*. Your thoughts, your ideas, your wondering.

If you are gentle with yourself, if you are quiet enough, if you *allow it* then ideas clarify. Things seem to flow again. Yes, you are still the same person.
Yes, you still have the same issues, problems, beliefs. But, they have had their hold on *what is possible for you now* loosened.
There is now possibility. For growth, for play, for more light and expansion in your life.

Where do you want to go, *today*?

Finding joy in unexpected places

Joy can occur in the most unexpected places.
A new beginning.
An old familiar routine or situation perhaps.

What is it that *you would love in your life*?

What is joyful for you?

When was the last time you *felt free*? You laughed perhaps? You danced, you sang, you ran freely down a hill?

What would you love in your life today?
What moment, when you look into your planned day ahead, could be *an opportunity for joy*?

CHAPTER 2

What moment or situation could allow some vibrancy? Some remembering? Some fun?
What moment or situation could you just stop in? Could you breathe in and express out?

Ask, " *Where is my opportunity for joy in this*? How could I do this, bring this, no - *allow* this, for me?"

Do you remember how free children can be? Yes, they have worries. Yes, you probably did in your own childhood, at least at some point.

But maybe, all this detailed super-safe, every-second-accounted-for planning is stifling *your opportunities for joy.*

Where is the expression? Were you even *allowed to do that* as a child? As an adult, a 'grown-up'?

Where is the fun, the joy, the connection in *your* life, *your* day?

Can you dare to imagine it? Imagine, consider, letting a little in?
Maybe when no-one's looking.
Maybe when you're alone.
Or maybe, just maybe *with another too.*

You never know. That may be just what *they are missing also.*

FINDING JOY IN UNEXPECTED PLACES

Let's run down that hill. Or roll down it.
Let's *play with this/that/the other.*

Painting, running, dancing, singing (no matter how 'badly').

Could you come home to *that part of you, today*?

Go on, I double dare you.

Which path shall I take today?

Which path shall I take today?

The one I took yesterday, when I looked after myself, cared for myself that amount? Or the one where I care for myself less? And others more?

Being a parent, a carer, a friend, a partner can all be beautiful, loving, yet also be draining and confusing at the same time. Often in the same day.

Can you remember how *you* felt as a child?
What were *your* relationships like? How much love, respect, self-honouring was there that *you were aware of*?

WHICH PATH SHALL I TAKE TODAY?

Often our perception of a situation may be very different to another's. Which, I wonder, is the most *useful*? Which, I wonder, would bring you the *most joy*?

Which way today then?

When you look back at your life, how has *your self-esteem* fared?
Has it grown or shrunk? Or maybe you don't know - you never thought about it before I asked you.
Could you take a moment now to consider?

Imagine asking yourself as a child. The adult you are now, safe and comfy, asking the little you. "How are you doing?" "Do you have everything you need?" "Would you like a cuddle, a hug or ... ?" "How can I help you darling?" "Would you, could you, let me give you something now *that you need*?"

Feel, honour, connect.

Then, when you're ready, back to adult you.

Did you enjoy this exercise? Find it interesting?
(If you didn't do it, go back now for a few moments and try again. It *will* be insightful and useful, I promise. *If you actually do it. For a moment is all it takes* to get benefit, insights ...)

So ... how was it?

CHAPTER 2

Did you try and dive straight in?
Was it easy? Uncomfortable? Horrible? Unbearable?
Or somehow reassuring?
Soothing maybe?

Time spent honouring ourselves and our *true present needs*
can be so empowering.
Listening to, hearing, asking about our *real deep needs*
can bring such *light into our life today.*

Could you do this for yourself?

Would you *want* to feel better, calmer, more relaxed?
Would you, *do* you, could you *allow* yourself to *feel*? Even
for these few seconds or minutes?

Taking time out like this to listen to who and *how we are*
today can make it *so much easier* to know which path to
take next.

When you have a deeper insight of *how* you are, you au-
tomatically know more of *who* you are too.

Be gentle and kind and *powerful* with yourself. You are
only one. You are here, in *your* life, now.

Where would you like to go?
How would you like to go now?

Do you take that path or the other?
Do you walk alone or with another?

WHICH PATH SHALL I TAKE TODAY?

These decisions, these wonderings, are *so much easier* to make when *you honour yourself, your deeper inner feelings, first.*

Good luck and tread gently with yourself. xx

Laying down on the side of the road

Are you laying down at the 'side of the road'?
Are you giving up on your dreams, your inner guidance and nudges?
Letting *your life* pass you by?

Will you look back at this time remembering *love* for yourself?

Or will you remember little, nothing? Just busy-ness. A time of 'stress', no power. No direction.

Can you dare to let *your light shine?*

Can you dare to look at, to remember, *all that you may be?*

LAYING DOWN ON THE SIDE OF THE ROAD

This is important. For this is where the real *living* happens. This is where you will *feel the most alive.* In *your*
life. Today.

What do you see in this picture?
Do you see life, or giving up?
Do you see only a dropped branch, a group of leaves,
dropped dreams?

Do you connect with the leaves reaching out into the sun-
light, finding, *claiming their* space in this world?

What is it that *you would really love?*
What is it that *those inner yearnings, those inner quiet
nudges, call you to do in your life now?*

Do you listen? To them?
Or only, mainly, the worries? The doubts. The "I couldn't
possibly" and "Who am I to think like that?"
The "I wish this was over now. Stop reading."
The "*That's silly. I could never do that.*"

It is actually up to you. You *can* breathe into this fear,
that judgment. That "I don't know if little me could ever
. . ."

Allow it to flow. *Allow* the feelings to surface.
Do you have a good practical friend or family member or
centred grounded professional who could help hold this
- the space, these emotional waves *while you are feeling
them, and you are held?*

CHAPTER 2

It *is* time. If you want it to be. If you *want* to grow, to learn. To live that *full life* that you dreamed of many years ago.

What step will you take in the direction of *your* dreams, today?

Go write it down. Write down *all the tiny little steps to get you there.*

Then begin. Then write, draw, paint, dance, speak, read, learn. Whatever it is that is calling you.
Take that first step.

You'll be so so glad if you do.

More importantly, you'll be so so so *you.* xx

Chapter 3

Standing out or blending in?

To stand out? Or to blend, to fit in?

Where are you in your life now?
Are you fitting in with the crowd?
Are you trying to copy, to blend, to emulate another, or two or three others?

Could you play with only being *you* for a while? Only for today perhaps. For *this one* hour.

How would *that* feel? Maybe take some time to watch your thoughts now. To consider a situation in *your* life, *where you don't feel very powerful, capable, loved.*

STANDING OUT OR BLENDING IN?

Who or what do you think of in that situation?

Can you *be in that feeling* for a moment or two? Who are you being then? Copying? Thinking, "I must, I *should* be like ..."

They know what to do, say, how to act. What choices to make.

They seem to know how to be there, or here.

But, and this is a big but, there is no space for two identical souls here. There never was meant to be.

How boring, how unenlightened, would *that* be? *Exactly the same?*

Where would the sparks be? The discoveries? The learning, the growth, the considering, discussing *and then expanding* in this universe.

Do you really want to stay stuck in the same place, the same vibration as another?

This planet doesn't need that. *You* don't need that. The time has come for you to expand into this light.

To shine brightly, on *your* terms.

Your reality.

Your *own growth* and path.

What is it that you have chosen to learn here?

Is it time perhaps to go into *that truth*?

To start to come home to *all you can be* and to *let that shine for all to benefit from*?

CHAPTER 3

Those who can benefit may stick around longer.
Those that it is not a good match for may move away.

You are more in *your light* now.
And that, my darling, can only be good in the long run.
Healthier. Freer. More fun.

If that's what you actually want of course? ...

Enjoy the journey. *Your journey.*

Come here into your heart one step, one day, one situation
at a time.

Then, and only then, will you feel fully loved. For it is
then, and only then, that you are loving you too.

I need to be different

I need, I should, be different.

Somehow, in some way, I ... should ... *change*.

In times like these, with thoughts like *these*, what am I
to *do*? WHO am I to *be*?
Should I stay little, small, scared, feeling somehow alone
(even though I *have* friends)?

CHAPTER 3

Should I be the superhuman-I-see-on-TV, in magazines etc?

Should I be them?
Should I? What a great question. And one that can lead you home to your heart. Your wellbeing-ness. Your *self*.

It is at times like *these*, with thoughts like *these*, that I wonder, "*Am I on the right path?*" "Am I on the correct *plan* for *my life?*"

"*Is* this what *I planned? Is this the 'way home'?*"

"*Am I 'getting it right' yet?*"

There is no time like the present to dissolve your self into *these thoughts*. These wonderings. These I-don't-know-who-to-be-now times.

For it is in these moments, these *precious moments*, that you try a different path. That you consider *new ways of looking at something*. That you, that I, and all of us can try out feeling, sitting with, and getting curious about who and what we are.

Do we *want* to go in that direction? Is that our dream or *someone else's*?
Is that my limiting belief or *someone else's*?
Is that *my* plan, for *my* life, or *someone else's*?

Is this, is *that*, what *I want in my life today? This week? This month? This time.*

I NEED TO BE DIFFERENT

Can you remember how to just sit and *feel*? To be in that place of not knowing it all. Of not knowing all the details.

And *that*, my friend, can be *all you need to do.*
All you need to have.
All you are, and more.

More of you in this space.
Less of *'them'* and *their* ideas.

More of how-can-I-be-with this?

More of can-I-remember how to be?

Can I remember what I wanted again? After all this chasing, this learning. This *trying to grow.*

Could I just sit with this?
Could I accept that maybe, just maybe, I am *enough already?*

That indeed I actually do have everything inside of me already.

That indeed it *is ok* to not rush, fix, create, be gorgeous ... just yet.

That maybe, just maybe, *this day, this time,* and *this* place of possibility, *is growing of its own accord, in exactly the right way and time.*

CHAPTER 3

Perfectly for me and *my* life.

I love you.
Love you too today.
Look in *your* mirror. Into *your* eyes.
For one minute today and feel what you see. And honour what you see.
And love all that *you* are.
Now. And for today. Only for today.

And see how *that* leads to you feeling, being, honouring.
If only for today, love *you*.

Is your climb too big?

Is your climb too big? Too far? Too insurmountable?

Is this actually *your* climb to be made?

Or perhaps is it *someone else's*?
Someone you saw on the TV or watched on a video? Or read their blog/posts/book or met them somewhere and thought, "*I must be more like that.*"

CHAPTER 3

Well, darling, maybe *this isn't your climb.*
Maybe you have your own beautiful mountain.

Maybe the view from the top, in fact from just starting to climb *that, your* mountain, will be so rewarding, so fulfilling, that you *don't need to go or be or do anything different.*

That maybe you are actually *exactly where you are 'meant' to be.*

That maybe, just maybe, you *are* doing ok now. You *are* all you need to be.

You *are ok already.*

Well then. What would *that* look like?
What would that *feel* like?
Can *you* imagine?

Could you *play* with this, in *your* mind today?

It may be fun. It may feel weird, but it sure is a lot lot better than living someone else's truth. Someone else's idea of what a 'good life' entails.

How would it feel to actually *get to the top*, to 'have succeeded', according to the TV/video/posting people? According to *their grace and beliefs and ideas and path.* According to what is *important and necessary and part of their life* for them.

IS YOUR CLIMB TOO BIG?

Well then, how would it feel to have reached and scaled and pushed and tried and then . . .

then, when you look around, you see it is *someone else's mountain*?

I am alone

I am alone.

Do you sometimes wonder this in your life? Out loud or silently at home to yourself?

In the shops, at the checkout, in a crowd at a party?

Is there a time in your life where you remember? Where you can just step back and see the big picture. The *really* big picture.
The view where you can *see* that in fact *you are not alone.*
You are *loved beyond measure.*

Can you, could you connect with this now?

I AM ALONE

This vastness. This emptiness. This space that contains all you are and all you ever could be.

This space that *is* yours, that *is you.*

A space that, as soon as you step into it, you remember, you reconnect. You say with your heart and feel with *all your body*, that yes, yes, this *is* me. This *is me.*

What colours can you see here? How does your body *feel* here?

What is it that *you want most in your life now*?
Could you use this space, this never-ending potential, to *visualise* it?

To touch, to smell, to *allow* it?

There is a wonderful power in our imaginations. A door, a gateway into possibilities. If we can *allow ourselves to dream. Allow ourselves to imagine. Allow ourselves to come home to that which really brings us joy.*

Then, then my friend, you can connect with the whole universe. And you are *never* alone.

Never.

And all the friends, companions, life buddies and en-hancers, life growers, life truly-support-you-to-developers pop in and naturally *gravitate towards you.*

CHAPTER 3

If, if you allow it to be so.

So flow today, sweetheart. Flow into this feeling of loneliness. Flow through and into the vast space of potential. Flow into fun and *your* imagination.

And then *allow the joy to come to and through you.* And then *you are not alone.*

Too hard to look at

Sometimes, when I'm 'busy', when I'm rushing, not quite sure where I'm going or even how exactly to get there, but I know-I-must-go, must move, have to ...

Then. Then am I busy? Do I actually *have* to rush, to do-lots-of-things? So many things. So much 'to do'.

Am ... I ... busy? Or am I rushing? Rushing for rushing's sake? Rushing to ... avoid. Rushing to ... run. Rushing to ... not know, not feel.
Not understand.

Where is this rushing coming from?
Is it my conscious thinking?

CHAPTER 3

Is it that in-the-dark unconscious, often unseen part? The part that seems to protect, to know, to look after my immediate needs.

The part that helps me manage day to day. That helps me cope day to day, with these *feelings*. These feelings that *I don't want to look at. I don't want to feel* thank-you-very-much.

I *don't want to* know, to own, to digest.

You are *not me*, I say. You are *not any use or needed here, in this space.* In this time in *my life.*

I'm managing just fine without you, thanks.
You *don't need to be here. You* don't need to be *here, with me now.*

But then, then there are those times when I *do* stop. I *do* feel. I *do* allow.

I *do* stop.

I *do* feel.

I *do* allow.

And that. That ... . What then?

What *do I* feel? What *do I allow*? What *do I know, then*?

TOO HARD TO LOOK AT

Could it be that *this is where my joy has gone*?
That *this* is where 'me' is hiding? The plans, the hopes, the dreams I had, I kept so well for so long?
Secretly, quietly, peacefully hoping that the conscious part, the I-can-look-at-you-now part would return. Would stop and be and rescue me again.

That I would *come home to myself* again.
That I would *remember it was worth feeling* again.

That at some point it *was ok to feel. It was.*

It was ok to know and feel and experience what is actually happening around me.

That *there was a time*, there was, when my life *was ok*, was safe. *When I felt safe.*

When we are children, we have such a different perspective on life, on our situation and safety compared to the adults around us. They *know* what is happening. They *know why* or when or *how we will do something.*

They can see the big picture. From our height, from the viewpoint and life experience of a child, thing are very different.
There *can be* more fear. More confusion.
More misunderstanding.

Different needs. Different wishes. Different hopes and dreams and perceptions.

CHAPTER 3

Maybe *we were* safe. Maybe we *were loved.*
Maybe it was ok. And safe. And love *was fully present in our lives.* Maybe.

When you and I were little, *we did not see so clearly.* So, when similar feelings arise, or are touched on, or even *glimpsed at* as a fully grown-up adult. Then, then it can be common to suddenly feel like that little child. To feel confused, overwhelmed. To feel OW. OW, *that's too much to feel now.*
That's too much to own. To live. To honour in my life now.
I can say, convince others, that I'm 'too busy'. "This is *far too important to stop* and look at *that."*
Look at *that.*
Feel *that.*
Honour and respect *that.*

For then I will (maybe) remember the 'horror'. Remember the 'feeling'. Won't I?

Can I? Could I? Could I *try* to come home to *that?*

Knowing that *that feeling,* this *honouring of that.*
That *maybe,* just *maybe,* you and I *could* do this.
We *could look.*

We could fail for a moment. And not be super successful. And not act as if we know everything. And say that "Yes, of course I'm fine. Why would you ask?!"

That maybe, *maybe it's ok to be human.* Not *super* human. That maybe we can *be kind to ourselves*, and *then* to others.

And *then* to our job, our home and those around us.

That *maybe it is ok to be me.* And that, *that is truly the most important decision I can make for me today.*

That I *can* listen (for a second). I *can touch the edge of this* (for a moment). I *can feel* into this space, for a fleeting second and *then see how I run. See how I run.*

And know, truly know that this is just a way of part of my brain trying to help.

It is ok to be me now. It is OK to be you now. That this is good. Ok. Loving, nurturing.

Don't you see that *this part of you is loving you*? You *are* loved.

Who would have thought? Who would have known that actually, in *all this time, you were and are loved*?

Who shall I be today?

Who shall I be today?

Shall I be them?
Or her?
Or him?
Or that fabulously glamorous/rich/enlightened/perfect . . .
(you fill in the blank to match your thoughts) that I saw
on the screen?

Should I be . . . ?
Should I be more . . . ? Should I be less . . . ?

Who *says this*? Who is it that is *thinking this*?

WHO SHALL I BE TODAY?

Is it *'me'*? Is it a part of me? A part that I don't see, don't know is actually *only a part of me.*

A part that maybe I can get to know. A part that tries to help. That *tries* to look after me perhaps. 'Helps me' to fit in. To get love ... and approval perhaps.
To 'be one of *them.*' To be *understood, valued, connected to* this outside world that seems so distant.
Out of reach. "*Not for me.*"

So then, *who are you being now, while you read this*? While you walk by yourself? While you read a book? While you worry?

Who are you being now?
How are you being now?
Anxious, worried, sad, upset, lost, found, vulnerable, strong, capable, believe-in-yourself? Or none-of-the-above?

Who would *you like to be*?

How about yourself? How would *that* be?
Wouldn't it, couldn't it be so amazing to *be yourself and actually like it*?

To be yourself, day to day, when you're with *that* person or in *that* situation?

Wouldn't that *be easier,* than *copying someone else's life? Someone else's path and journey* (and 'issues' - we *all* have them)?

CHAPTER 3

Do you know that *you cannot be anyone else better than they can? Or anywhere near as good as them?*

But, and this is the fantastically freeing part, you are the only one who can be the best you.

And you do remember how capable and great you are, right? Did you remember? Could you?

Play with this. Search your life, your memories and *find that time. Find the evidence.*

There are always many memories, many ways to view yourself, but, but *you can choose. You can choose which to focus on. Which to grow and nurture and love and honour.*

Which, which of all your great and tiny victories, will you choose to focus on today?

Peace is in your heart, if you let it

Peace is in your heart, if you let it. If you let it be there. If you let *yourself be there.*

Yes there is joy. Sometimes pain. Sometimes laughter. Sometimes clarity.
But what is it that *you* are seeking? What *is it* that *you wish for*, want, desire, *need in your life* now?

Who is it who 'put that idea in there'?
Did it arise from within? Forming of its own accord and then coming into your conscious awareness when you sit silently alone?
Did it arise from a magazine, a post, a book? From *someone else's* idea, thought, need, wish?

Where is peace for you? Is it somewhere that you reach often?

Does it "depend on *who I'm with*, what *they* say. How *they treat me*"?

Does it? Does it *really*?

Who is that you are seeing when you look at them?
Is it them?
Or is it a reflection of what you say to yourself, perhaps every day of your life?

Are *they* enough? Are *you* enough?
Do you see how *this can become blurred*?

The great, really powerful, thing is, *we cannot fix another and it change what is inside of us*.
We cannot 'fix another' and it 'solves' how we feel.
We cannot (try to) fix another and have it change anything in our own heart. Truly.

There is only one person, one soul if you like, *in you*.
It is *your* needs, *your* wishes, *your* hopes and dreams that need to be attended to first.

Then *it does not matter* what the other does, as much anyway.

It *does not matter* how much they love or admire or *need* you.

PEACE IS IN YOUR HEART, IF YOU LET IT

You are you. Alone or with company. You are you.
And that, that, *that is enough (already).*

There is a fight going on inside of me

There is a fight going on inside of me. Inside of *my* body. Inside of my *life* perhaps.

"I *wish* ... I *regret* ... I *own* (or at least *try* to)...

I am ... There are ... We should ... They *should have* ..."

These are all ways of *avoiding the truth*. *Your* truth. Your *ownership of your self*.

Your *ownership* of what you *can* be. What you *could* be. *Can* you?
Could you?
Could you *be* all that *you* are?

THERE IS A FIGHT GOING ON INSIDE OF ME

Can you *let the river of your life flow?*

Can you dive deep into *your* depths?

The fresh clean cool water of possibilities. Via the muddy waters of doubt, fear, insecurities and I-am-not-enough ideas.

Through, and into, your *self.* Where *you* lie, rest. Where the thinking I'm-in-charge part says,
"There's no-one there. There's no-thing to see there."
"Keep on moving, attention. No point stopping to examine (or play with) *that.*"

But maybe there is. There *is a point. There is* some one, *some thing worth looking at.*
Some thing, some place that contains *joy.* Contains *life. Contains excitement.*
Yes, and pain on the way. And fear, and joy, and many many emotions and moments and doubts and I-don't-knows.

Hmm. So do I, do you, *play there?*

Do I, do you, examine, look, *turn our attention in, into there?*

For there, *maybe you will find your truth.*

For there, maybe you look and see yourself.
The little you. The big you.

CHAPTER 3

The I-don't-know-what-to-do-with-my-life-yet you. (Remember that one. She'll probably pop up again. xx) Maybe, just maybe, *you* will find *you* there.

In that 'hole' that appears full of no-thing-ness. Full of an empty lost emotion.
Maybe, just maybe, in *that darkness* there is you.

And there is no need to fight. No need to fight. That maybe all you will actually find is more of you ...

And a reunion can occur?

Do I have to leave my body?

Do I have to leave my body? To be like ... you, or *that?*

Do I have to be some *one* or *thing* else? *Or how someone else is?*

Do I have to tune out of, away from, my soul? My love? My being-ness?
Who I *want* to be? *How* I want to be?

Do you remember ever feeling or thinking like this? As a child, as an adult, maybe this week at any point?

Sometimes we feel great 'like' for ourselves. Occasionally maybe great love. Other times, maybe more often than not, we're thinking, "I should ... " "*They* have got *it right.*" "Maybe I'm not ... enough." "Maybe I should ... more?"

Do *you* connect with *this?*

Do *you want* to be different?

Different to that *pull.* That *drive.* That I-should-be-something-else-now. Some how different.

Well then, maybe it's time to stop being *so hard on yourself.* So *limiting and restricting* on all you *can* be.
On all your *beauty.* Yes, you read that correctly (see, you *can* do *something* right).
All ... your ... *beauty.*

Now when you hear *that* word, what is it that *you* are thinking of, feeling, seeing? Is it the *outward image* that is projected *so much* in the media?
Or is it that *place of peace*, of *enough-ness* that *can* reside in *your* heart, *your* body, *your* life?

Is it? Is it? Could you *be there* for a minute, or two?
Could you own your own body? Your own life? And your wishes, and hopes and I-don't-dare-to-dream-that-out-loud thoughts that come and visit sometimes.

Could you? Would you? What about if I told you *it was ok* to do that?
It is *ok* to be *you.* It is.

DO I HAVE TO LEAVE MY BODY?

Can you actually *really be anyone else right now?*
Can you actually be *that* person? *Their* life? Or whomever or whatever it is that your thinking, worrying, not-enough-yet thoughts/ideas say to you "I should be ... "

There *is* a place for that. There *is*. But it's called acting, playing, dress-ups, pretending, role modelling.
It
is
not
now.
Not *real life*. Not who you *planned to be*. *Not*, if you get *really honest and really quiet with yourself* (in a place where no-one can see or interrupt your thoughts), *who you are.*

Who, what, how would you LOVE to be? To express?
To know again?
To welcome into you and *your* life?

Where has *she* been hiding? Isn't it great that *she is still here? Still around you. Still available.* Yay.

So say "Hi", get reacquainted. Maybe go for a walk together. Or paint together. Or write or play or dance together. What's fun *for you now?* What *first comes to mind?*
Then *go ... with ... that ...*

Go with that my love. And the homecoming gets all that much sweeter.

CHAPTER 3

Have fun, learn, grow, fall, get back up again.
But, most of all, *have fun.*

Time for a change?

Shall I always do it *this* way?

Is it perhaps time for a change?

Time to move *into this emotion.* Time to *let it all catch up with me.*
Time to move on. Time to stay?

Can I remember what this was all about anyway?

When we stop. We listen. We *allow.*
We *allow all those parts of us,* thoughts, beliefs, ideas, concepts we formed early on to come back into our conscious awareness. To say "Hi".
To get 'back in the picture' again.

CHAPTER 3

Well then, what is there to do?

Do I *love* you, *honour* you? Let you *be here with me?*

Or do I, as is often the way, skip over *that* feeling? *That* idea? *That* wish, or hope or dream?

Do I, *can* I, allow it to blossom? To catch up with me? To swarm in around, between and *with* me?

Do I *let myself see* all those things I think I did 'wrong'? *Those things* that "I won't go and look at that again, ever.
They can stay in the past thank-you-very-much. *They* can just randomly disappear.
I ... did ... not ... see ... you. You ... are ... not ... with ... me ... now.
You ... do ... not ... exist.
Thank you. Now go away.
Go back down where I push you, keep you. *You do not need to be here, with me.*"

But. But. But. How is that working for me? For you?
Is this something, a life path, that I truly want?
Is *this* the way I want to *live my life?*

Is this the way I want to *come home each day?*

Am I really being *kind to myself?*
Am I taking as good care of myself as I wish, I want, maybe demand, that others do?

TIME FOR A CHANGE?

Is this what I want? Is it time for a little no-one-has-to-see-this-just-yet change?

Could I maybe, without telling anyone? Could I maybe, just maybe, listen to it?
Listen to that part of me (yes me) that is trying to catch up? That is trying to reintegrate and make me feel whole?

Is there a way to do this that feels ok for me now?
Can I give *myself* what *I* need now?
More rest, more good, more quiet, more fun, more noise, more laughter, more ... ?

Do I actually need to be different, stronger, fixed, successful, *have their permission* first?

Do I? Could I?

What about now?

Is it time, perhaps, *to let that part of me that I have not listened to, honoured for so long, to pop over, sit next to me, enter my chest and feeling space. To be with me and it's ok.*

Getting the support I need. Giving myself a few moments quiet *somewhere.*

Maybe turn the screen off for a minute, or three?
Maybe go for a walk and sit somewhere, alone?

CHAPTER 3

Maybe, just maybe, I could *be with myself for a moment, and that would be ok.*

Is there a way (to be with you)?

Is there a way to be with you and not lose my *self?* Is there a way to be around you and still remember who I am, what I need?

When I put your needs first, when I *try to please you,* and meet *your needs*, wishes.
Then, then *where do I go?*
Why does my sense of me go? Vanish? As if it doesn't matter.

Why have *I started to do this?* There must have *been* a start, at some point.
It wouldn't make sense that I was *born* like this. Or everyone would feel the same, right?

CHAPTER 3

So *is* there a way *out* of this? A new way of thinking perhaps? A *new way of approaching* a situation. A new, another way of *being around someone.* Where I am not lost. I am still present. Do I need to give up on *my* needs to meet *yours?*

In this thinking pondering space, we can begin to get back in touch with *ourselves. Our* light. Our wishes, and needs and desires.

How can we truly, really, *honestly,* look after another *if we are not well first ourselves?*
How can we help another spirit to evolve, to self love and nourish and nurture, *if we are not willing to 'do the work',* *act it out ourselves?*
How can *I* show *you* how to be, to live a joyous healthy life, *if I don't do it for me too?*

"How *can* I love myself then?" you ask.
How *can* I?
Who are you not to? Who are you to stay small and stuck and little? Unimportant.
What about all your skills and love and cleverness and useful ideas?

Do you *really* want this 'small-ness' for *your family?*
Do you *really* want *them to stay small?* Ambitions un-realised? Potential unmet? Soul and light and spark unexpressed?
Joy gone into hiding "for another day", another 'time',

IS THERE A WAY (TO BE WITH YOU)?

another ...?

They will do it if you do.

They will love themselves, and you, if you do.

("But *I* need ... . But first I have to ... . But they should ... ")

They will remember what their plan was, where their joy was, find their light and spark, if you do.

If you do.

Yes, this can seem hard, impossible maybe. But what is, what *is* your alternative?

The end?...

I am enough already

I am enough already.

I am big.
I am strong.
I am very capable.
But I don't always feel this way.

Am I capable? Yes, you are.
Have I 'achieved' enough already? Could I consider having a day off, *some* time off? No pressure, no 'thing' to achieve. No-where or place to go. No destination or final goal?

I ... am ... enough ... already.

I AM ENOUGH ALREADY

Today, right now, I *know* this. I *feel* this.
What is the difference *today, now?*
Why and for whom do I feel or think *differently?*

What is it about today, *now*, that *leads me to feel this?*

There is only time and space between these different ideas.
Different ways of *seeing me.*
There is no difference in my skill set, my real experience,
my knowledge. Today, or later this afternoon.

So what is it, what *is it* that gives this idea of enough-
ness? *Allows it to be here, within 'me' currently?*

Is there a separate part that comes and goes? Is there
another person in there, in 'here'? What is it? What is
it that is allowing *this particular feeling today?*

When you come home to *all* you are, all you *already* are,
then settle. Then *be with it all.*
Yes, yukky-I'm-not-so-sure-I-like-that bits.
Yes, the bits you *would* choose if you could, the parts you
show others early on in your relationships. Yes, those bits
that "actually I'm rather proud of".

But those, those, *those are all outside judgements. Outside* viewpoints. *Outside* criticisms or ideas of worth, va-
lidity.

What is it that is important to you?

CHAPTER 3

What is it that means the most to you?

What are *your* values, what *you* consider admirable qualities or those that meet *your* ideal? When I use the word ideal, I do not mean the glamorous 'ideal' we see in magazines, on our screens, in other's pictures or posts.

I am only, only, *only* talking (well writing actually) about those qualities that come from *your* inner integrity. Those values that *mean the most to your soul, your heart.*
The values that, if you were to truly live by them, would make *you feel proud.*

You would feel proud.

When you *know* it is good, and honest and truly true *for you.*

Not another soul's path. Not another person's view of glamour, or success.
But one that comes from that quiet solid part.
The quiet soft voice or feeling that feels right to you, feels peaceful and loving perhaps and *only has your best interests at heart.*

Maybe you need to get out alone in nature to feel it. Maybe you feel, or hear, it when you are immersed in water. Or playing or running freely. Or resting after a challenge?

Maybe you haven't felt it for a while. But it is there. It *is there.*

I AM ENOUGH ALREADY

Go on, take some quiet time out today. Go for a run, a walk, a swim, *whatever calls to you now.*
(That's the thing to really do.)
Get to that little quiet I'm-here-to-help-and-love-you voice or feeling.

Those ideas. Those feelings. Those times are what form the foundation of you knowing you are enough.

You ... are ... enough ... already sweetheart.

Will you *allow this feeling* in your day today? Will *you* let it form in your heart, your inner knowing? In your belief or theory for today? *Your* day.

Holding on to feelings

Shall I 'hold on' to this feeling? Or 'should' I let it go?

Can I be with it, allowing it to blossom, to show itself to me? Or shall I let it remain in darkness? Hidden in some way in my subconscious. Hidden from my view perhaps, but maybe still seen, observed by others.

Can I let the light of my attention fall gently, softly onto it? Could I let it rise up from my depths?
From my storehouse of pain or insecurity?

HOLDING ON TO FEELINGS

From *that place*, that place that keeps me 'busy'.
"Sorry! Too busy for that … to stop and do *that*".

Could I allow the light of my awareness to let it come to
me? Perhaps when I feel safe, with others around. Or
perhaps when I am alone with myself.
Perhaps when I have - or can easily get - a journal or
notepad, a pencil or pen. Then just write.

Just write.
Write whatever is on my mind right now. Whatever
comes up to meet my awareness. Whatever is saying,
"I *want this!* I *need* this!"
(Or maybe what it *doesn't* want.)

Maybe what you came here to do is to look at that. To
give love to that feeling. To re-nourish the *whole of you.*
Warts and butterflies and all.

Is there somewhere to 'go' with that? Is there a place to
be? A "super-flash-I-am-healed!" kind of destination?

I don't think so. I don't think so.

I think maybe, maybe if I sit with this. If I let my beautiful self show me *more of what and who I am already.*
Then, and this sounds good to me, then I could remember my wholeness, my light, my Being.
And love and fun etc *will* be there. *And I am too.*

And I am too.

Chapter 4

Can I remember where my heart is?

Can I remember where my heart is?

Could I take a trip there, just to visit, even if I did?

Could a taxi take me there, for a fleeting pass by? A "Hi, haven't seen you for a while" brief visit. Just to check. Just to know *you are still there*.

If I *want* to, I could. If I *wanted* to, I *could do anything*. But maybe, maybe, I don't. I don't *want* to look, to feel, to know. To remember.

Perhaps I *don't want* to do *that*.

Perhaps I only want to 'keep busy' now.
Perhaps I *don't want to* look, and feel and *know that I*

CAN I REMEMBER WHERE MY HEART IS?

am not perfect. Most definitely not whole, or loved, or needed or appreciated just as I was. And am now.

But maybe it is *not their job anymore to love me fully.* Maybe it is. Maybe it is *not their job now* to appreciate me and *all I have become.*
Maybe I could *do this alone? I could do this with and for myself?*

Maybe I could do this *with your help.* With a *currently alive or present adult.*
Someone who *is* strong. Who *is* capable. Who *can look after themselves,* without me there worrying about them, caring for them, *holding them nearly every second of the day.*

That may be how it feels to you now.
That may be how it is. For you, *your* experience.
That may be all you have *ever* known - or at least that's how it may feel.

There *is* hope. There *is* light. There *is* love.

And the great thing is you can do this for yourself.

If you *allow* love.
If you *allow* nourishment.
If you *allow* others to help *you. Now. Today.*

Could you reach out?

CHAPTER 4

Could you learn to 'let go' of this need to be 'right'? This need to be 'ok'. This need to say "I can handle this" or "I can't".

Whatever it is that is *your* story. Whatever it is that you tell *yourself*, to get you through *this* day, *this* time, *this* moment in *your life*.

Does it *feel* like your life? Is *someone, something else* in charge? Leading, choosing, making choices for you?

Can you remember where your heart is?
Could you have a *little* look today?
A *little* play, or visit, or drive by to say "Hello"?

Could you bring yourself home *from your heart?*
Could you bring yourself *to* your heart?

Could I, and you and anyone else who feels like this, start to own, to remember *our own hearts?*
Today. A little. Then maybe tomorrow a little again.

Then a day or two off.

Then a little again.

Oh there you are. There. And actually, when you *do* look, when you *do discover* . . .

You will find that you have actually been you there, all along.

Inwards first

Inwards first.

When I'm wondering where to go. When I'm pondering "What *should* I do now?"

When I'm unsure of the next step or which direction I *should* take. Then, and many times then, I go in.

Inwards first, *before* the decision.

Inwards first, *before I can see.*

Inwards first, *before I know myself enough.*
Enough to feel, to hear, to acknowledge where and what and *how I am just now.*

CHAPTER 4

What I *need*.
What I can create just now. In this time.

Where am I meant to be? No-where.
What do I need to do? No-thing.
What am I meant to be saying, achieving, *knowing* now?

When these questions come, these queries, these I-need-to-know-now wishes, ideas and pressures. More theories and ideas, *from the outside. My* outside.

Then, then, then. Then it *is* time. Then it is *time*, to go, to search ... *within.*

Turning inwards, towards my heart, towards the silence underneath the chatter (*my* chatter), the inner thoughts, ideas and concerns.
Underneath the 'front' I put on. The I-do-actually-know-what-I'm-doing image.
That I *think* I'm portraying sometimes. And at times that *is my* truth and it flows so naturally.
And at times it doesn't.

But *is that enough?*

Is there, *can there be*, a part of me, an *inner* knowing, that *knows* this? That *sees* this?
That *feels this 'I-am-enough-ness'.*

That *knows that coming inwards is the best thing for me now.* That *knows* home is *only, truly* found inside.

INWARDS FIRST

That *knows*, until you find your *own* heart, your *own* feelings, your *own inner-ness*. Then there *is* no home. There *is* no peace.

Only patch-ups.

Can I turn in now? Can I *be with myself* now? And *know*. And know, that *that is enough*. I am. You are. We are enough *already*.

Is this my home or someone else's?

Is this my home? Or someone else's?

Is this where *I* live, or someone else's ideas, theories and beliefs?

Who is it exactly that is driving my fears? My wishes, my hopes, my *dreams?*

Who, or what part, *allows* this? *Allows* me to feel, or not.
To believe, or not.
To stop and listen to that super joyful part that knows.
That knows.
That knows.

IS THIS MY HOME OR SOMEONE ELSE'S?

It *knows* what I truly need. It *knows* what I actually want - that part of me that doesn't often show itself. That doesn't, *that often*, come up into my vision. Into my heart, my awareness, my *understanding.*

Can I, can you, *allow this now?*

Can we *see what this is really about?* See what part of our vast lifetime of memories this is stemming from? Real or not. Imaginary or not. Alone, or not.

Who is it that you are living now? Who is it that you are *being* now?

Who is it, that *you want to be* just now, in *your* body? In *your* life? In *your home* that you call a body?

Can you phone home *now?* Can you 'pop home' for a visit *now?*

Could you at least write a postcard?

"Hey there, it's me.
This is what's going on for me at the moment, what *I'm* doing (busy, busy, busy).
Can you let me know *if I can bring you anything back?*
Can I *post anything?* (Time to yourself, to rest and nurture yourself? Quiet time to be heard and received and *acknowledged?*)

... Well, that sounds interesting.
I'll see what I can do, body.

I'll see what I can manage/carry/build-up (or maybe, just maybe, *let go of*) to help with that. *To help with that …*

Lots of love,
Busy mind and 'achiever'

P.S. Be home soon (probably) xx"

I don't want to ...

I don't want to ...

I don't want to feel *this* so I'll fix *you* instead.
I don't want to go *there* so I'll blame *you* or *that*.
It wasn't *my* fault. It wasn't *that*.
It was ...

Anything but what is *really* happening.
Anything but what is *really going on*, under the surface.
Under *your* surface.

Is it real? Is it?

Do *they/it really need* what you are offering? What is it
that you are offering exactly?

CHAPTER 4

Is it a way *for them* to 'feel better', to 'get what they need'?
Or is it maybe, a way of *you* getting what you need, or want, or would like?

Is it perhaps a simpler easier way to say that, "Something *else* is the problem, not *my* problem"?
Is it perhaps a way to say, "Yes, that's what *they* need/want/desire when actually *it is all about you?*
Or rather a clever-by-your-subconscious way of *avoiding you?*

A clever-by-your-subconscious way of saying, "No, sorry. *Far too busy* to deal with/sort out/heal *that* now." *Far* too busy.
Far too something-else-that-sounds-important (you fill in this bit for your story).

Story? Story. Hmm, yes. A story.
A way of talking to myself that feels ok. That validates, maybe excuses, how I'm really feeling.
A way of living, acting, talking and being that lets me 'off the hook'.
That lets me pretend for a while.

And no, these times may not happen often. *You may not feel like this every day.*
(You may not, I may not, be *aware* of this anyway.) But they *are still there.* They are still *here.*

I DON'T WANT TO ...

In *your* life. In *your* home. In *your way* of being, of *living now.*

What would *you* like? *What would you love,* actually?

Is there a place, a moment in your day, today, where you can pause and say "yes" to *yourself?*
Where you can *honour* that part inside of *you* that really needs a "Hello, hi, how are you going at the moment"?
A part, *the part, that remembers all there was, all that happened. All of that.* And how *awful it felt.*

Then my friend, my clever loving-yourself-now friend. Can you open the door on that *part of you* a little?
Can you say, "Hi, how are you? Is there *anything you need* now? Can I *help you, in some way, any way*, just now?"

Then listen. Then trust. Then hear.
And love yourself, with kindness. Gentleness. And love, again.

You are. You are whole. *You are still alive. You* are here *now. And that is enough, for now. Enough.*

Love. Love. Love.

You are here

You are here to *do* something.
You are here to *be* something.

Can you remember? Can *you remember* what, with whom and *how that may be?*

Can you remember what your *plan* was?

What did you wish for, as a little girl or boy?
What did you *love?*
What did you *play* with?
Ah yes, to play. To play, to play, to *play.*

So many of us have forgotten *that.*
Forgotten that *yes, that is part of the plan too.*

YOU ARE HERE

Part of why you are here. *Part of* what you wanted, came for, needed and requested.
Part of your *soul's* journey.

Did you *like* to play then? Do you *like to play now?*

Are you actually *allowing* this part of *your* life to develop? To *exist* even?

What *is it* that you *crave?* What is that you *wish so deeply for* when you are alone? When you are with your thoughts? *With your feelings?*

What is it that speaks to you at night when you can't sleep, or when you wake briefly?
Or, even better, when you first awake? When you first awake *by yourself.* Naturally.

Has that actually happened in a while?

Is there anything, *anything* that you can think of that *could* help with that?
It is a special feeling to catch that moment, those *moments of insight.* When, upon first awaking, you can *hear your soul's journey.*
You can *hear, and feel and know,* even if only for a few seconds, why, what and how you are here.
What you *truly* need and desire *in your life now.*

Not what someone else says you 'should' do.
Not what someone else thinks is 'best for you'. "What

you need right now is ... " "What is *most important in our culture* now is ... "

... meaning, "Please don't change. Please don't grow or then maybe I'll have to consider that too. *I'll* have to consider that maybe *I'm* not content/at peace/ok enough *now too*. Please don't change or then I may have to."

Yes, change can feel uncomfortable.
Yes, growing can initially feel a stretch, a big stretch perhaps.

But what is it exactly that you want?

What is it exactly that you n*eed, desire, wish for* in your life today?
What is it that pulls so strongly at your 'heart strings', at your desires?
What is it that you wish for now?

Is there a path?

Is there a path? A way *back home?*
Could you see if you did stop and look? Stop, pause, take a breath and look?

Could you see how *you have been running from yourself?*
Could you see that? Could you listen for a second, one second, to *your heart?*

To that place that *knows* you?
That *loves* you?
That *is* you?

A place, a precious special holding-on-to-lots place that *needs you here with it.*

CHAPTER 4

That needs you to be here with it.

It calls out sometimes. Sometimes when you *are not look-ing.*
When you are *not 'here'.*

What is it that you remember when you stop?
What is it that you feel, when you *are* alone?
When you *do* have friends, but you know there *is a place*
for busy-ness. A place for holding on.
And a place for not knowing too.

What are you coming home to, today?

Why is it the hardest thing?

Why is it the hardest thing to ... ?

What is this for you? Today, for me, this is about honouring myself.

About honouring *me* when I am in *that situation*, when *that* issue is arising. When that 'button' is being pressed. When *that feeling* is arising, coming back up in my life to say "BOO!"

Why is this the hardest thing? To find, to take, to *ask* for something? For now, for me, this is for time alone. For one of 'my walks'. For quiet time to reflect. And to remember who I am, what I was, and what I *can be*.

CHAPTER 4

This is about *allowing* time, *allowing* self-love, and honouring and nurturing and 'all those things' you are *meant* to do. To be, to create, to solve.
To just keep going/doing/moving/fixing/solving.

Is it *really* ever *enough?*
Is there *really* any time to just be, just sit, just feel?

And allow. Allow light to come back in. *Allow* clarity and sanity to arise out of the I-must-do fog.

And when I'm here, and that's *all there is*, then, then, then, *that's all I know. All I know.*

And when it isn't, when it isn't. When there *is* light and clarity and love and laughter and fun and joy then yes, yes, I do *not know that.* I *do know this instead.*

So which is real? Which is valid, important, *actually real life? Which is actually here and how, or maybe even who, I am now?*

Which is real?

Which is *me?*

Which, what, how shall I *be* now?

Do you know me? The one who sees me so often. Or do you see only the front, the current experience or feeling?

Do *you see the whole?* Do *you* see all I *can be?*
Do you see who I really am?

WHY IS IT THE HARDEST THING?

These are questions that come up when I'm really in it. *In* the emotion. Lost maybe, no clear sense of self or what is theirs and what is me, my 'stuff'.

There can be so much blurring of these concepts, especially when we get 'triggered'. When something someone does, or says, or writes, or shows us, produces a *very intense emotion. A very intense response.*

What *is it* that we are reacting to?
What is it that *throws us so off balance?*
What *is it* that we are *feeling?*
What *is it* that we are holding on to, sharing, expressing, *not loving?*
Not enough yet anyway.

Is it really *you* that I am *solely reacting to?*
Is it maybe *me?*

Is it in fact an old story, a memory or experience of an old event that is *just too painful to look at again? Just too painful* to examine, to look at, to hold, to love, to honour? *To digest?*

What is it that you *truly want in your life now?* What is it that *you truly desire?*

For this answer, for your *real* answer, you *must go in.* Go in to 'open the door to', to say "Hi" to that part that stays closed off. That part of you. That *part*, part of *you*.

CHAPTER 4

Is there a way to go in? A way to go in that doesn't *result in pain*, or tears, or remembering *those* feelings?

Maybe, maybe not. I *only* know that when I *do* make time, when I *do* dare. Then I am always, *always* rewarded with some peace, some deeper understanding. Some deeper understanding of myself *and* the other. *Who* am I seeing when I look, and get triggered, *there*, in *that* way?

Is it perhaps time to come home? To this, to you, to love?

Is it maybe time to get some help? To say, "You know what? I *can't* actually manage all this myself. I *do* need, *would love*, some help now."

Could *you* do *that* for *you?*

Does success have to be conditional?

Does success have to be conditional? Does it have to be based on x, y or even z?

Do I have to know 'how much I am worth', how much I 'can achieve' before, before, before I can ... ? Sit down? Relax? Earn? Receive? *Allow?*

Can I sit with my-*self*, just as I am now?
Maybe *not* the 'brightest flower'.
Maybe *not* the 'most-beautifully-perfumed rose'. Yet.
Maybe, maybe not.
But *can* I be ok with that *now?*

Can I be ok *not* knowing? *Not seeing all that lies ahead in my future.* In the future of those I care for, spend my life with, see on a day to day basis?

Can I *be with them, just as they are now?*
Do *they* have to 'be perfect', 'be successful' now too?
Whatever *that* means.

Can I *be with me* today? Just now? *Just now.*

And *that*, that is enough.

That ... is ... enough.

Is there a time for joy?

Is there a time for joy?

On my morning walks I've been brave, I've been bold, I've faced 'stuff' - stuff I've probably been avoiding for years.

But what about facing joy? What about *that* feeling, *that* emotion, *that way of being?*

Yes, being brave with your 'stuff' is so *important*. Yes, listening to your innermost deepest hidden feelings can help you connect deeply with you.

But so can joy. *So can joy.*

CHAPTER 4

Where *is* that, in *your* body?

Do you *have a sense of that?*
Do you *want* to? Have *time* for? Even *remember* what that *feels* like?

This is so *important.* This *feeling,* this *emotion, this part of your life.*

I've *tried* to be brave and feel and listen and know. And yes, *that is important,* and necessary.

And yes, this *can be a powerfully transformative time.* But there is *also* joy. *Also fun to be had.* Times to just play, and dance, and laugh and be silly. *Be silly.*

Hee hee, ha ha. How long is it since you did *that?* With *them?* Or by yourself ... *by your-self?*

For this, this, *this also brings you home.* This also helps you *remember who you also are.* Who you also can be and feel and how.

Is it time to come home to fun, and daftness? Is it time to get out your bike, or rollerblades? Or just sit on (or even better roll down) a grassy hill?
Is there a favourite uplifting fun song you love you can think of?
Go find it, get it out, *put it somewhere you can access it easily, and quickly.*
Then play it.

IS THERE A TIME FOR JOY?

Play it.
Play ...

And begin to remember what, who and how *you can also be*.

My son put a sticker on my shoulder this morning

My son put a sticker on my shoulder this morning.

Did I make time to pause and listen to his request, his suggestion, his *fun idea?*
Did I make time to pause and *receive his gift?*
Did I make time to pause and receive *him? And then me, to me, for me too.*

This is the important stuff of my day today. *This* is the precious moment, an *insight into joy* that I've been missing.
So focused on my 'goal'.

MY SON PUT A STICKER ON MY SHOULDER
THIS MORNING

So focused on 'achieving', getting 'somewhere', that I forgot to *see the beauty*.
See the beauty that is *already here*.
That ... is ... already ... here.

How lucky am I? How lucky and honoured do I feel (or *allow myself* to feel) that *this time, this gift,* is being given *to me?*

Is there a simple gift that is waiting, or maybe already being offered to you?

A sunrise waiting to be watched?
A park waiting to be played in?
A favourite drink to be made and savoured?
A cuddle, a hug, a call with a friend or partner?

Could you make a list now of the *tiny gifts, even opportunities for gifts*, that are in your life already?

In your life *already?*

Do I acknowledge you?

Do I acknowledge you? Do I acknowledge that you are here, with me, inside my body or thoughts? Inside my mind, behind my decisions, in front of (and sometimes hiding) my desires?

Do I stop to *see* you, *feel* you and *know that you are here, with me today?* In my thoughts and worries and confused times. Within and without my choices - or at least those I *think* I make.

Is there ever a time when *you will not be here?* Will not be *with me?*

Is there, will there, *could* there be a moment when *I see you,* for all that you are? *All that you are.*

DO I ACKNOWLEDGE YOU?

Is there a time today when I will *not remember you?* Not *see* you? *Not acknowledge you exist?*

Is there a time when *I am ok just being*, being me, being with a friend or partner or child or colleague?

Is *this* a day where you begin to dissolve? Where I *feel* you, *acknowledge* you and, at the same time, *know that you are not all I am made of?* Know that *I am more than 'just' you?*
More than, *so much more than*, 'just' you.

I am a child (in memory, in laughter, in silliness) AND an adult.

I have experienced and known (and *remember too*) joy and laughter and silliness.
I *remember* love and appreciation and fun and *an inner knowing that I am enough already too.*
I ... am ... enough ... already.

Already.

Already.

Me too.

Can I stop hating myself, *blaming* someone or *some thing?*
Can I pause for a moment, and *know that I am enough already?*

CHAPTER 4

I am enough already. I am. You are. *There is no-where to go*, to be. *No-thing to have*, or own or create.

Right now. Just here. Just you, and *your body. Your life.*

Can you *be with that* just now, for only today?

Only today . . .

When you are growing

When you are growing,
breathe into your heart.

When it feels too much,
breathe into your heart.

When you *don't want* to be here,
breathe into your heart.

You *know you are home already* when you take time to
do this. *Make* time.
In fact you could do it right now, if you wanted to, *dared*
to. *Allowed* yourself to.

CHAPTER 4

Or
just
do
it.

Just do it. Breathe *now*, in and out *now*. *Look at* this feeling, this opportunity, this *freedom*.

How easy is it to create it just now? For you?

Can you go in, *dive* in?

Feel and accept?
Feel and *accept*. Feel and accept.

There *is* nowhere else to go at this moment. There is *only in*. So let's go. Let's look, let's *feel*.

What ... what ... what are *you* feeling? Feeling when you stop and go in?

When you breathe into your heart?

Let's sit on the edge of that. That taste of overwhelm. That edge of fear and can't-go-there.

How bad is it, *really?*
How ... bad ... is it?
Put it on a scale of one to ten. From not noticeable to overwhelming.

There, you got something. You got some *information*. And, and this is the *really great part*, as you observed, as

WHEN YOU ARE GROWING

you measured, as you *felt and looked and explored*, then, then my darling *you are not your pain.*

You are you, observing.

You ... are ... you, watching, seeing, glancing, understanding.

And *then* the love comes.
And *then* the clarity comes.
And *then there you are.*
There you are.
And it's ok. And you are home.
And it's ok, *you* are ok (and still standing and alive and x, y or z *hasn't* happened. *It hasn't.*)

And there you are, my sweetheart.

There you are.

What is it you want from your life today, sweetheart?

What is it you want from your life today, sweetheart? What *is it* exactly you are seeking?

Can you pause, breathe, stop for a moment and *feel* this?

Could you go to a window and look at the sky? Could you take a minute (just one little minute) and go outside and *lay on the grass?*

Then, then, then. Then tune in to your thoughts, feelings and *wants*.

I *want ... .*

WHAT IS IT YOU WANT FROM YOUR LIFE TODAY, SWEETHEART?

I *need* ... .
I *think* ... .

What is it exactly that you are saying *to yourself?* To your self? To you?
To the one that is *always* present. Is *always* with you, talking, saying, *sharing* what it thinks, knows (or would like to). What it owns, *is in charge of* (or, at least, would *like* to be in charge of).

What is it exactly that you are saying to you?

More to 'achieve' perhaps?
More to know, to own?
More to be, to have, to want or to 'acquire' perhaps

Is that ... is *that* what you *really* want?

Is that ... is *that, what you are seeking in your whole life now? What you think you absolutely-must-have/know/be now?*

Is ... that ... *useful?*
Is that the *best way of loving you now?*

Is that the best way of *coming home to you now?*

To all that you are and *can* be.

To all that *you* are and *may* be. If you allow it.

If ... you ... *allow* ... it.

Thank you for reading my book. I'd love to keep helping and inspiring you ...

Sign up for special offers and to find out when my next book in this series is released at www.beccyhowe.com/books

Follow me on Facebook @BeccyHowePage
Follow me on Instagram @BeccyHowe

Join the conversation in our Facebook Group "Journey to Serenity"

See you there. xx

Notes

Notes

Notes

Acknowledgments

So many thank yous, to all the following:

To my wonderful family. You have allowed, encouraged, given space for, inspired and assisted me in becoming so much more that I would have alone. I love you, I thank you, my family.

To my wonderful editing friend Robyn Swanson. You were, and are, a joy to work with. Thank you for sharing your wisdom and knowledge whilst encouraging and allowing mine to also shine. Thank you to my journey pals Sue, Hannah, Denise, Elaine too. Your support and grounding over these past years have provided a rich and fertile ground for us all to grow and shine. I love and am so grateful for our special times together.

A huge thank you to all the trees I have sat under, gazed up at and, of course, hugged. To the many beaches, grasses and rocks I have pondered, wondered and laid on, thank you. The grounding, the solid reference, the real presence and peace you all provided me with was life-enhancing and changing. It still is.

To all the people (and dogs) I meet on my walks. Your conversations and connections have helped me stay (mostly) joyous, grounded and present.

To all rainbows past, present and future for lifting me and helping me to see the possible light and potential in each moment that you share with me.

To Australia for providing me with such a rich backdrop of space, positivity and beautiful nature (and delicious food!) which has allowed and inspired my inner yearnings to bloom into this world.

Thank you to the many professionals who have inspired and motivated my path. By sharing your own tools and journeys you have made it much easier for me to share mine. These include Wayne Dyer, Doreen Virtue, Louise Hay, Oprah Winfrey, Elizabeth Gilbert and Marie Forleo, to name a few.

And, of course, a huge heart felt thank you to the little (at first) part of me that didn't want to feel, to go there, to be brave but did anyway, and then shared it! I thank you, honour you and love you with all my heart.

Lightning Source UK Ltd.
Milton Keynes UK
UKHW050422270221
379477UK00006B/47